GRADUATE WRITING

10 Simple Habits for Writing the Perfect Graduate Paper

Graduate Writing: 10 Simple Habits for Writing the Perfect Graduate Paper by Alvin Bush Denver Colorado,80222

www.graduatewriting.club

© 2019 Alvin Bush

AB.Method.Writing@gmail.com

Coverd by Alvin Bush.

ISBN: 9781082083266

DEDICATION

There are two reasons that I wrote this book. The first reason is because of the love that I have for my family. To my wife Grace and our children, I love you all with everything that I know is love. I want this book to be a living testament of my work, perseverance, and dedication towards constant self-improvement. To my children, let this be an example of how believing in yourself, working hard, and staying focused on your goals can create anything that you can imagine. I love you.

The second reason that I wrote this book is for all of the underdogs out there like me who were not born of privilege or pedigree. We were forged in the fires of rural Michigan, Virginia, Ohio, Florida, Georgia, Colorado, Washington, Arizona and in the urban jungles in Chicago, Baltimore, Los Angeles, New York, Detroit, Boston, and all over America. We understand that hard work and determination is the only way to survive in these environments, and that education may provide a way to improve our chances. We are the ones that were told that we would never be anything more than what other people thought of us and our environment. This is to you. I want you to become the best writer that you can be and prove to yourself and the naysayers that they were wrong about you. The world needs to hear your story, but you are the only one that can write it. Love is love.

Alvin D. Bush

10 Simple Habits for Writing the Perfect Graduate Paper

Too Busy to Write the Perfect Paper?

Are you trying to balance work, school, family, and social life just to find yourself looking at a blank screen just days before an assignment is due?

Have you ever had a busy week where it seems like everything is due by weeks end and there is just not enough time in the day to get everything done?

Now it's Sunday morning and there is a five to ten-page paper that is due at midnight that you haven't even started on. So, you rush to piece something together hoping that it will be enough to get by with a passing mark. Realizing that you appear unprofessional and untrustworthy by turning in your writing assignment late and with so many spelling and grammatical errors that you begin to panic and doubt yourself.

Trust me you are not alone. Many of us attempt to balance all of the many aspects of our life only to find out that for many of the things that are important to us we are barely getting a passing mark. I know this is true because I was once the person that was described above. I too struggled to balance military life, school, and family and I was barely getting a mark in any of those categories.

One of the hardest things about writing is just getting started.

There are many intimidating barriers that will prevent you from taking the first steps, or when you do finally take them you feel a huge burden to get something of quality in by a firm due date. This book removes many of the intimidating barriers that lead to poor writing habits and it offers my proven strategy to successful graduate writing. This method that I have designed is called the **AB Method of Writing**.

The **AB Method of Writing** is a methodology that I developed over my academic experience to help me streamline the process of writing through the use of technology. Utilizing this method, it allowed me to remove many of the common barriers to writing and enabled me to perform at a high level consistently. This tried and true method is what I used during my Master's degree to write efficiency and effectively.

The best advice that I can give to a college student, graduate student, or someone who is simply looking to improve their overall writing skills is to take small, realistic, and achievable steps towards improving their writing over time.

This book primarily focuses on the graduate experience rather than the undergraduate experience, however, the lessons from this book can be easily applied to any stage of your college or professional development to help you become a better writer.

* Remember that the goal is to be a great writer by the end of the degree and that being a stellar writer on day one is not a strict requirement to start or continue your educational journey! *

These 10 habits are excellent because they are simple to understand, and they take very little time and effort to begin to use. As you progress through your educational journey, you will begin to see how your peers and professors begin complimenting you on your writing ability. Your skill will be on full display when they recognize you as the go-to person in helping other people improve their writing!

For example, Simple Writing Habit #2 of this books suggest that to become a great writer it is essential that you first **pay attention to the required writing style of the course or style needed to capture and maintain the attention of your audience.**

This simple task requires minimal effort; however, research shows that this is one of the most common mistakes that students and others make when beginning any writing project. By making this a writing priority you will build a strong foundation for the framework of your written work.

Educating yourself about the writing style of the class or project that you are tackling is the most important step that you can make towards successfully completing your goal of becoming a better writer. The next step involves an awareness of the tone of your presentation and knowledge about your audience's level of understanding about the subject you are presenting. By being able to convey your research accurately to your audience and identify the correct language that is needed to convey that message, you will have a powerful strategy and a powerful voice in your writing that will transcend other students in your cohort. This understanding will act as one of the most powerful tools that you can have as a future scholar.

"Always Remember That You Are Either Succeeding as a Writer or Learning How to Become a Better One."

– Alvin D. Bush MHA

These are the small things that you can create for yourself that will have lasting effects not only within academia, but this knowledge also translates over into your professional life and career. By having the tools needed to be a respected scholar and feeling a new confidence in your ability to generate brilliantly written and coherent works, this will give you the energy, and edge to tackle any assignment or project in your path. As you make these incremental changes you will get the results that you desire, and in time you will be able to create the perfect graduate paper.

IS THIS BOOK FOR YOU?

Most traditional teaching methods of writing involves an overemphasis on the highly technical aspects of writing and often lead the reader to become more frustrated in the process even before they have started. Those methods rarely lead to better writers, but instead, it creates a lot of stress, self-sabotage, and anxiety about the process of writing or even pursuing higher levels of education.

These conventional methods don't fully address the underlining issue for most people these days of time management, nor does it appreciate the fact that we live in the digital age where we can leverage technology to create more meaningful and impactful written works. The reality for many people is that they are trying to get these assignments done while juggling their 9 to 5 job(s), other classes, and their family or social lives. The truth is that you don't have an infinite amount of time to read some 355-page book about becoming a better writer. For most of us, the only objectives that we are trying to achieve include displaying a level of understanding about the subject that is assigned, get the assignment done efficiently without too much hardship, and to get it turned in on time.

My approach to writing simplifies and structures the process in a way that will help you to build skills over time through repetition and expand your capabilities through the use of technology already available to you for **free**!

Therefore, I will say that if you are someone who is looking to have someone else writes your paper without you contributing any of your personal knowledge about a subject or pay some internet service to write papers for you…this book is <u>not</u> for you. Integrity, self-improvement, self-respect, and learning from my mistakes are at the heart of everything that I do. So, if you are someone with these same values, take the challenge to build up skills that nobody can ever take away from you, and I promise you, you will be successful.

So, whether you are pursuing a bachelor's degree or entering a graduate program, understand that this time in your life will be both exciting and strenuous, but you should look forward to the journey and the challenge ahead. Although this book was written primarily for the graduate student it is also applicable for students entering high school, college, graduate school, and those individuals that just want to improve the clarity of their writing. Be sure to highlight the section titled "Automate Your Correctness". In this section, I will give you *3 **FREE TOOLS*** that are the secrets to my writing success.

Congratulations on this new and exciting journey! This book will teach you some of the methods that I used during my master's degree to help me write clearly and professionally while meeting the page number and structuring requirements of each assignment.

LET'S GET STARTED

Let's begin that perfect paper by developing those habits which lead to the greatest success with the least amount of stress.

Be sure to pay close attention to those technical sections throughout the book, as those sections will be invaluable in developing a templet which will make implementing this new strategy even more effective as you take the steps towards becoming a better writer.

Now, let's jump into this book and discover the 10 Simple Habits for Writing the Perfect Graduate Paper which will help you to begin your journey of becoming the best writer that you can be today!

HOW IS THIS BOOK ORGANIZED?

I've designed this book to be easy to use and highly effective, and by utilizing my approach this will improve your writing in no time!

I've structured this book to focus on 3 graduate writing elements that highlight the core approach to writing the perfect graduate paper. These elements are easily digestible and act as a guide to helping you to take the next steps in becoming a graduate level writer.

Each element is further broken down into 10 simple habits each, which include an action plan for each of these sections. When all of these aspects are used in conjunction with your previous knowledge and experience it will take your writing from that of a student to that of a scholar!

These 3 elements and 10 Simple Graduate Habits for Writing the Perfect Graduate Paper are listed below. Enjoy!

CONTENTS

WELCOME TO GRADUATE SCHOOL!

Welcome to graduate school you did it! All of the hard work and dedication towards pursuing your dreams of having a Master's degree has finally paid off. You should very proud of yourself and you should relish at this moment and understand that upon completion, you will become part of a very exclusive group of people that have reached this level of education. Congratulations!

SO, WHAT'S NEXT?

Attending graduate school requires a big commitment and at this phase of your education, it will demand much more of your time and knowledge than did your undergraduate studies. Writing and research will compose much of the requirements and benchmarks of your program, and you will need to successfully progress through each element to show comprehension and mastery within your academic program. Writing academic and scholarly papers makes up a significant part of any graduate program and your ability to write efficiently and effectively will constitute a significant part of being successful in your graduate program.

Your assignments will require you to write from multiple viewpoints and each will ask you to incorporate a broader perspective than what you have previously been asked to present.

The goal of this is to build the students perception about the world around and help them build a higher order of thinking while incorporating diverse ideas. Moreover, as a graduate student, you will be expected to cultivate a range of different writing styles to be able to present to a variety of different audiences across a scope of numerous topics within your field of study. These attributes I what I later understood as the fundamental difference between that of a student and that of a scholar.

GRADUATE WRITING ELEMENT #1: STUDENT TO SCHOLAR

STUDENT: *is a systematic and attentive observer of action with a pursuit of knowledge.*

SCHOLAR: *is a systematic and focused facilitator of advanced concepts within a specialized field of study.*

As you are beginning this journey you will find that you will be transitioning from that of a student to that of a subject matter expert, leader, and scholar within your field of study. The key to becoming great lies in your ability to be clearly understood when communicating your ideas to others.

In business, the one skill that is lacking the most in my experience is the ability to write clearly and communicate effectively. In an age of hashtags, short hands, and tweets people want to say more with less, but I feel that it is more important to write clearly and effectively with just enough words.

The key thing that you want to focus on when you are writing is clarity. You need to be able to clearly define your topic and establishing a methodology in understanding what is needed to convey your idea or research topic before you even begin to write your paper. The following questions will help you organize and structure your work so that your writing is both clear and concise. You should ask yourself:

- ❖ What topic do I want to write about?
- ❖ What information do I already know about this topic?
- ❖ Where can I find additional resources and information about this topic?
- ❖ Who is my audience?
- ❖ How will I structure and format this paper in accordance with the guidelines set by the professor?
- ❖ What will my final work look like when I am finished?
- ❖ What will my research and writing contribute to my field of study?

Addressing these questions in every assignment will help you develop the habit of organizing your thoughts into an effective methodology that will help you successfully structure and write your paper.

GROWTH TOWARDS LEADERSHIP

Realize that you will be asked to be a leader throughout this process, and it is upon you to make the decision to capitalize on this opportunity. For this reason, I placed this element at the beginning of this book because it is the most essential attribute that you will need in helping you to establish yourself as a leader and expert within your field of study. Your ability to organize your ideas and communicate them successfully to your desired audience will make your journey through this part of your education easier and more enjoyable.

"Everything that can be said can be said clearly"

(Ludwig Wittgenstein)

Now, let's have a look at Simple Habit #1 to see what we can do about overcoming some of these writing challenges.

SIMPLE HABIT 1:
TAKE PRIDE IN YOUR WORK

Great writing skills are a crucial component of nearly every profession, and your ability to clearly and accurately convey a message can be the difference between success and failure, life and death. For instance, the medical field involves a lot of technical and time-sensitive information which is passed throughout a network of people and machines. Doctors are required to take very detailed notes about a patient's condition then relay that information to other staff members to ensure that the patient is properly cared for and that the patient's chief medical complaint is remedied. The pharmacy staff receives prescriptions from providers and then must reinterpret the information to make sure that the dosing instructions are in line with the recommended therapeutic dose before dispensing the medication to a patient. There is a lot of information that needs to be communicated accurately to ensure success, and the pride that comes with receiving, executing, and distributing information and services accurately, is at the heart of every successful medical treatment facility and business.

Nearly everyone in the world utilizes e-mail and text messaging to send or receive information, and the importance of a first impression cannot be understated. Whether you are sending or receiving communication to or from your managers, work colleagues, partners, or clients, your ability to clearly document, and communicate those interactions will depend on how successful you will be within that organization.

There have been many research studies that focus on social psychology and the importance of a first impression. When mistakes are made, or the message is not communicated clearly, research shows that it takes serious work to repair or undo what was communicated. This can mean the difference between being taken as a serious professional or not. As a graduate student and eventual leader, your knowledge and expertise will carry with it the pride, accountability, and responsibility of a leader and scholar. Make sure that you take this new role seriously and success will follow you.

Action Plan:
Commit yourself to the future version of you. Think in your mind's eye of who you would want to become and take pride in becoming that person. Take pride in your ability to write and communicate effectively and you will be amazed at how much simpler the process becomes. Always remember that as you write and communicate with others, you never know who may eventually see your work and become a fan of it.

Now, let's move ahead to Simple Habit #2. This section focuses on the different types of writing styles needed for graduate school.

SIMPLE HABIT 2:
UNDERSTAND THE ASSIGNMENT
AND WRITING STYLE

During my college and university experience the common reason that I would see people fail or do poorly on an assignment is that they didn't really understand the assignment nor the format and as a result, their work was in the wrong format and in the wrong style of writing.

Whether you are in the school of business, science, anthropology, or communications be sure that you understand the professor's required format for the written assignments and the writing style of your paper. There are many different ways to format your paper which include MLA, APA, or Chicago Style, just to name a few. Your success in this area will be highly contingent on your ability to quickly and accurately identify the recommended format and present your findings in a concise and easy to understand way. Now that we have touched on the format of your written work let's move on to identifying the different types of writing styles.

Now, there are four different styling methods which are used in writing which helps you explain your topic. Those four styles are Descriptive, Expository, Narrative, and Persuasive writing. Understanding these different styles will be key in demonstrating your ability to adjust to the various assignments that you will be asked to complete. Let's look at each of the four styles of writing to gain a better understanding of the individual components that create each styling method.

Descriptive Writing

The first style of writing that we will address in this section is the Descriptive Style of Writing. As its' name suggests, the descriptive style of writing focuses on describing a situation to the reader or audience that enables them to visualize what the author has experienced or researched. This style of writing is very commonly used in journals or descriptive essays. The main purpose is to describe a situation in a highly-detailed and accurate way. The idea of this style of writing is to evoke all the senses to allow the author to visualize what is seen, heard, tasted, smelt, or felt during an experience. This style can also be used to describe an event, a character, or a location in great detail.

Example:

In descriptive writing, the author will not just say: "The basketball star hit the game-winning shot."

The author will change the sentence to focus on the details and descriptions, to convey the emotion and excitement of the moment to the reader. It will instead read something like: "The shot hung in the air for what seemed to be an eternity, while the piercing eyes of the red-eyed assassin knew that his shot would not miss it's mark.

The shot heard around the world, struck fear into the heart of his enemy as they knew that this bloody saga and their reign has come to a brutal and bitter end. The game ended with a new king and new champion."

Now that you have a firm understanding of the descriptive writing style, let's move on to the next style which is Expository writing.

Expository Writing

The Expository Style of writing is one of the most common types of writing which is frequently used in most business, technical, and scientific programs. The main purpose of this style of writing is to explain a method, process, or procedure. This style focuses on providing the reader with scientific evidence, statistical data, and research diagrams. The structure of this style often follows a logical and sequential format with the goal of explaining the author's research.

This style is primarily subject-oriented, and it emphasizes informing the reader about a specific topic without voicing the personal opinion of the author. This style of writing is essential when the author is trying to present information to a mixed audience in a scientific way without personal bias or political spin.

* Note: When you are in a graduate program for Business, Health Science, or Information Technology you will definitely need to understand this style of writing because, in my experience, this style

of writing will be the bulk of what you will present to your professors and peers. *

Okay, now that you have a better understanding of Expository Writing, let's move to the next section which is the Persuasive Writing Style.

Persuasive Writing

Unlike Expository writing, Persuasive writing contains a lot of bias, rhetoric, and opinions of the author. This style of writing is very commonly used for letters of recommendation to get into graduate school, cover letters, letters of criticism, opinion-based editorials, blogs, and reviews.

This style of writing focuses on convincing the reader to agree with your perception and stance on a given subject. By providing them with specific reasons, arguments, and justifications about their perspective, the author seeks to build consensus in order to bring about a call to action event. This style of writing is a very powerful tool in marketing one's ideas to a company, a professor, or peer group during your graduate journey.

*Note: Companies pay high salaries to individuals that are able to master this style of writing. Your ability to convince people to buy a product, service, or idea is invaluable in any field of study that is pursued during your graduate experience. *

Okay, now that you have a better understanding of Persuasive Writing, let's move to the next section which is the Narrative Writing Style.

You are doing awesome, Let's keep going!!

Narrative Writing

We have arrived at our fourth and final writing style which is the Narrative Writing style. Common examples of Narrative Writing include short stories, novels or novellas, and biographies. The main purpose of this style of writing is to tell a story about an event or person. This style of writing can be both fiction and nonfiction in nature. The significant difference between the narrative style of writing and the other forms of writing rests in the ability of the author to create different characters and illustrate what happens to them throughout the story.

I see this distinction in the way that this style doesn't only concentrate on informing the reader or audience about a specific subject or fact alone, but it focuses on entertaining the reader and having them buy into the point of view of a specific character within a story.

This style of writing takes its narrative perspective from that of one of the characters within a story, which is known as the first-person narration, and follows them through their experience throughout the story. These stories have characters and dialogue which are presented in a format which chronicles their journey from the beginning of the story to the end. These stories often have action, drama, horror, or another conflict within them which increase the experience for the reader.

Moving Forward...

Each of the four styles of writing focuses on the different stylistic elements which helps to convey the author's message, and this is one of the most important aspects of writing. Your ability to freely transition from style to style will allow you to speak to a broader audience and distinguish yourself as a brilliant writer. Be sure to review this section as needed to help you identify which style best suits your intended message and audience.

Action Plan:

Make sure that you reach out early to your professors to have them clarify any assignment that you don't understand. By doing this early in your education it will help you become more comfortable with asking for help from professors and peers. Make sure that you know what is being asked of you and how to create those deliverables early in the writing process.

At the graduate level, you will definitely need help from others particularly if there are group assignments or project. Next, you will need to identify the common writing themes that appear within your degree coursework. For example, if you are a business major most of your written work will be in APA format. Identifying the theme and format will save you so much time during your degree coursework.

Lastly, please be sure to reference this section as a resource to identify the writing style that is appropriate for your audience. Developing these habits will ensure that you understand and are able to deliver what is required of you during your educational journey.

Now, let's move ahead to Simple Habit #3 which focuses on the importance of starting your assignments early.

SIMPLE HABIT 3:
EARLY BIRD GETS THE WORM

The old saying that the early bird gets the worm, is as true as it is today, as it was 50 years ago. When I was in the military, we exercised the habit of arriving to every scheduled event 15 minutes prior to its scheduled start, and if you were on time you were considered late. By adopting this strategy to every part of my life, it has proven to be one of the most important habits in setting myself up for success. I found that there is nothing that can better prepare you for success than preparation.

I am a firm believer in the fact that the earlier you start the earlier you can finish. Finishing early is important because it gives you time to review your paper in a meaningful way and ensure that what you are presenting is something that is of value and quality. There are many research studies that demonstrate the power and effectiveness of creating multiple drafts of a project prior to submission. Research studies have concluded that your ability to refine your written work multiple times before submission significantly increases the quality and professionalism of your presented work.

The Beginning of Graduate School

The excitement of the first day of graduate school is exhilarating. You say to yourself, I finally made it, I am going to show everyone that I deserve to be here, and I'm going to do a great job, Yea! Well for me, that excitement lasted about a semester before I realized that I wouldn't get across the finish line by adrenaline and caffeine alone. I needed to set a schedule and stick to a methodology to be successful in this arena.

It is easy to be excited about graduate school for the first 90 days, and I have seen many students share in that excitement and enthusiasm. However, as the program progressed, I started to see them less and less until I eventually never saw them again.

What I realized is that in graduate school and in life, success is the result of persistence and perseverance over time. Represented as a mathematical formula it would look like: (persistence + perseverance) / time = level of success. Over time I found that it's not the person that is able to sprint through life to get a check in the box that are the most successful, but those that are methodical, persistent, and deliberate with their intentions that builds success that can stand the test of time.

A theme or idea that will always remain true in graduate school and in this life is the idea that ," Real work has a long shelf life."

As a result, the strategy that I created hinged on the fact that I needed to commit myself to starting my writing assignments early (often times the same day as the assignment is given) so that I could stay on top of the workload and execute at a high level. By adopting the early bird habit, you too will find success and stand out as someone who is on top of your game in graduate school.

Action Plan:

After class, write down what you already know about the assignment you will be writing about and what you will need to research in the future. By doing this as soon as you get home it will ensure that you at the least are putting something down at the beginning stages of gathering your ideas and framing your project. Make this a habit for each class, each session, and each assignment and success will follow you throughout your graduate and professional journey.

Next, let's move on to Writing Element #2 where we will discuss how technology and traditional writing methods intersect.

GRADUATE WRITING ELEMENT 2:
TECHNOLOGY & TRADITION

"Time is the Wisest Counselor of All."

- Pericles (495-429 BC)

The importance of utilizing technology to help you create great written works cannot be understated. I can remember my time as a young student learning about the many writing components that make up the English language and the different roles that each play when making up a body of work. What I found throughout my education was the fact that the tradition of writing and the way that we teach English in the digital age has not evolved with our advancements in technology.

The method in which we create, consume, and critique content has changed due to the rise of web 2.0 and social media outlets like Twitter, Facebook, Snapchat, and Instagram. These platforms have redefined how we think about what we say and how that is communicated to a worldwide audience. As businesses continue to shift towards an increasingly tech-based style, hiring an individual with powerful writing skills is essential to the success and longevity of that business.

So, whether you are sending emails full of typographical errors, grammatical errors, or poorly constructed sentences, how you are perceived as an employee and professional is on display. Your peers may attribute your lack of precision to a lack of education or a view that you are lazy and that you take a similar approach towards your work. Therefore, having great writing skills not only improves how you communicate within the workplace, but it can also have a positive effect on how you are perceived by others within your organization.

In the next three sections, we will address these concerns by setting up and enabling components within MS word which will help us to more effectively utilize technology to our advantage. In these sections, I will reveal many of my secrets to simplifying the writing process while also helping you to identify grammatical weaknesses within your writing. I can't wait to show you these simple habits which helped me to create and review a lot of quality content within a short period of time.

Now let's move ahead to Simple Habit # 4 where we will focus on developing a habit that I use to help me generate content quickly through the use of technology.

SIMPLE HABIT 4:
USE TECHNOLOGY TO YOUR ADVANTAGE

Have you ever had a time where you knew what you wanted to say and had everything ready in your mind but was suddenly distracted, and you completely forgot what you were going to say or write? Whether it's a pop-up ad on the phone alerting you to the latest gossip on Twitter, or a loved one distracting you with idle conversation, there are a litany of distractions that can happened which can make you completely forget what you were going to say or write. Or better yet you sit down at your computer and have your ideas ready to go but you start to type, and your fingers can't keep up with your ideas. Therefore, you slowdown your thoughts in an attempt to correct this error, and it results in a complete change in the language of the paragraph?

Sure, we all have. This dilemma is why I sought to find the simplest method to express everything that was on my mind before I was distracted or forgot the idea or concept. This is why I wanted to find the simplest way to execute this process, and what I found changed the way that I approached writing forever, and hopefully, it will change your approach as well.

The technology that I used is referred to as dictation or speech to text technology. We all have this technology available to us on our phones and on our computers. Dictation allows us to capture all of those thoughts that we have about our topic and the computer program will write down everything that we speak into it.

* Please note: When using the dictation function on either your phone or pc please be aware that there is a delay. Meaning that you will need to speak a little slower for the computer to be able to build a database of your normal speech pattern and translate it into text.*

So, I used my phone's voice to text function within Samsung note to speak about my ideas and how I understood the topic. When I finished talking about what I knew about the topic through research and my working knowledge, I would then send the dictated note to my e-mail address and copy paste the text into the section in MS Word that I was working on.

Action Plan:

Start to familiarize yourself with the voice function on your phone and computer. Next, use this function to make a to-do list for today. The more familiarity that you have with this function the more time you will save in building your paper in the future. As your proficiency continues to increase and the software begins to recognize your speech pattern, you will be able to fully integrate this technology into your creation methodology. Now, let's move onto Simple Habit #5 which continues the theme of using technology in writing.

SIMPLE HABIT 5:
AUTOMATE YOUR CORRECTIONS

Use technology to your advantage!

We are living in an age of technology that I could only dream about as a kid. We have technological tools available to us that are often free to use. Let's unlock these free tools and figure out how to use what we already possess to our advantage. Listed below are the _**3 FREE TOOLS**_ that I used to automate the grammar and punctuation process of correcting my graduate papers.

These free tools saved me a tremendous amount of time and energy in revising my projects and writing assignments. These _**3 FREE TOOLS**_ are: Microsoft Word autocorrect function, Microsoft Spell Check function, and Grammarly.

The first two free tools that you have are found in Microsoft Word. Microsoft word is great at catching grammar and punctuation errors in your writing. With automated functions like auto spell check and sentence structure recommendations, this provides us a great advantage in correcting our papers as we are writing them. However, this by itself isn't enough to properly edit and correct your paper. You will also need the third free tool which is Grammarly. You will need to download the free Grammarly extension to your version of Microsoft word so that you can have this third level of auto-correction available to you.

How to add Grammarly extension to MS word.

Grammarly is a free service that has upgradable paid features, however the free version will help you out tremendously while you make the decision to upgrade or not. Please click on the secured link below to add the Grammarly extension to your MS Word program.

* If you have other writing platforms that you use instead of MS office, be sure to check www.Grammarly.com to ensure that they have your program of choice. *

Windows / Mac - https://www.grammarly.com/office-addin/windows

* Note: The links will allow you to download the Grammarly extension for Microsoft Word only after you create a profile. Grammarly doesn't require you to enter any credit card information, it only requires you to set up a free profile. *

Once you have downloaded the extension it will appear on your MS word toolbar as demonstrated below.

Grammarly Functionality

Grammarly provides recommendations for the errors that it identifies within your writing and provides a recommendation for correcting it. The software also provides the reason that it identified a section in your paper as one that needs revision. It is as simple as clicking the green recommendation and Grammarly will change it within your paper. You are also able to click ignore and Grammarly will go to the next error. See the example below.

One thing that helped me to become a great writer was the fact that I paid attention to the recommendations that were made by Grammarly as well as the grammatical rules that applied. I focused on remembering those rules that flagged errors in my writing, and with the goal of not making the same mistake in the future, I overcame simple and complex errors in my writing. Over time Grammarly identified fewer and fewer mistakes as I progressed as a writer.

Action Plan:

The goal of this section is to develop a habit of checking your paper with MS word functions like auto-correct as you are writing your paper, and then have Grammarly check it again at the end of your paper. By doing this you will be able to catch all the common errors that people make with punctuation, spelling, and grammar. Now, let's go on to the next section where I will give you another free and valuable tool in polishing your final work and creating the perfect graduate paper.

SIMPLE HABIT 6:
READ ALOUD 2.0

As we discussed in the prior section, having your paper auto corrected and Grammarly corrected will help you in finalizing your paper. Once you have structured your paper and corrected all of the errors, the next step in the process is to have your computer read your paper back to you. By having your computer read your paper back to you it will ensure that what you wrote is what you are trying to convey. Often times when people are asked to proofread their own paper, it becomes very difficult to identify errors because our brains are wired to fill in the gaps in most cases. The brain often times looks at the entire word rather than the individual letters that make up the word. For exmple, see if you can raed the pasasge below:

" The oredr of the wrods in a seteance are not iprmoetnt nor are thee leatters taht meke up the wrods as long as the frist and lsat ltteer aer at the rghit pclae!"

WERE YOU ABLE TO READ THE PASSAGE?

See, the mind is often able to fill in the blanks to convey understanding without the need to observe accuracy. If you were good, you would have been able to read the passage with ease. If you were really good you would have also identified that I misspelled example (exmple), read (raed), passage (pasasge) before I introduced the example to you. If you were able to catch all of the errors, then you are an all-star!

HOW DO I COMBAT THIS BIOLOGICAL ADAPTATION?

Traditional writing practices advise that you have other educated people read your paper and give you feedback. This process has worked for a long time and is still an excellent method for reviewing your paper. However, in this modern age of technology and constant distractions, I found that there aren't many people that had a lot of time to review their own projects and papers, nevertheless review and provide feedback for mine. Therefore, I found a way that would help me to get the experience of having someone else read my paper without the need to have an actual person read my paper. The solution that I found was the **"read aloud"** function that is built into the Microsoft Office platform.

THE READ ALOUD FUNCTION.

The "read aloud" function is binary in nature as it will only read exactly what is on the screen. This ability to have the computer read exactly what is written without bias is by far the most beneficial aspect of Microsoft office that I have used during my graduate studies.

In many cases, I thought that I had finished my project, but as a habit and last step I would use the read-aloud function to hear what it sounded like when it was read without a biological filter. What I found in some cases is that what I was writing was not always what I was trying to convey. During graduate school I understood that often how you say something is more important than what you say. This is especially important to remember in situations where your written work will be presented to an audience. Utilizing this function will be the 3rd step and final screen for correcting and finalizing your written work.

HOW DO I SET UP THIS FUNCTION?

Depending on the version of Microsoft Office that you have will indicate whether you will have to enable this function or simply locate it on the toolbar and start using it.

First, we will walk through step by step instructions on how to set up and enable this function. Later we will locate this function on the toolbar for newer versions of MS Office and discuss the pros and cons of each method.

Here are the steps to setup your device and allow you to begin utilizing this feature within Microsoft word.

Steps to set up these features within MS Word:

Step 1: Open Microsoft Word and select a new blank document.

Step 2: On the top toolbar, right click on the review tab.

Step 3: Left Click, Customize Quick Access Toolbar. This selection will pull up the Word Options table and allow you to customize the review tab.

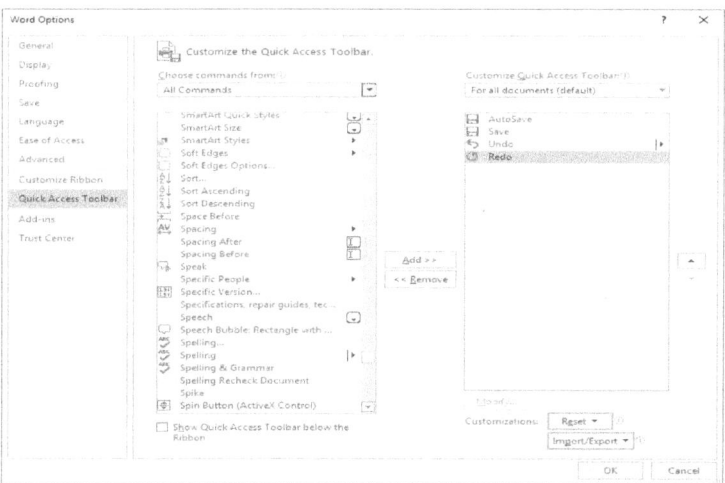

Step 4: From the Choose commands from the drop-down menu, be sure to select "all commands" from the drop-down menu.

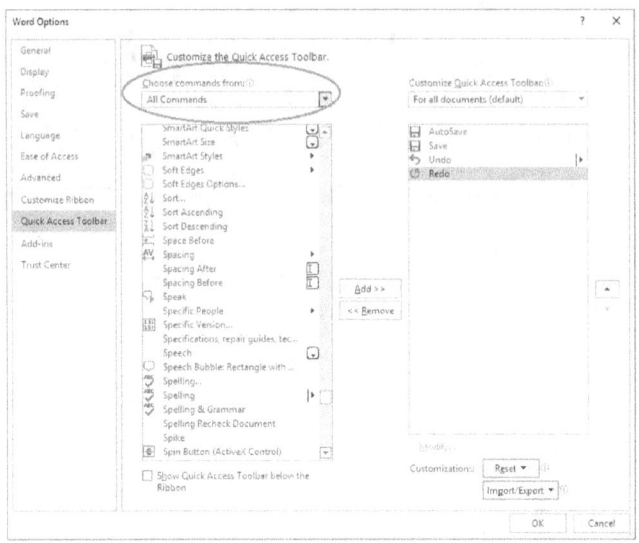

Step 5: Once you have enabled all commands, scroll down the left side menu to find the speak function.

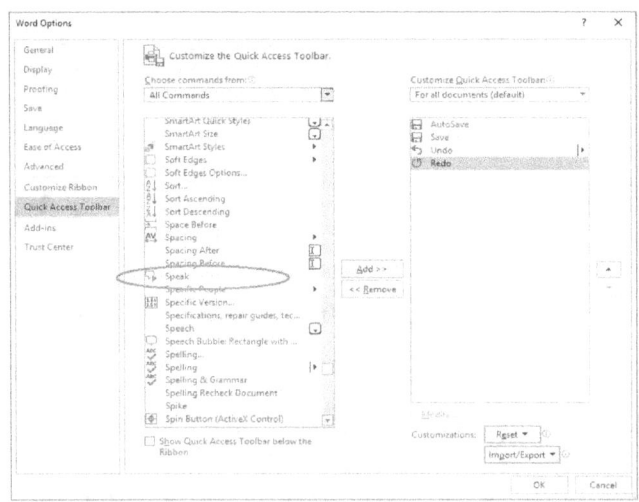

Step 6: Left click "Speak" to select the speak function. Then left click "Add" to add it to the review menu and then left click "OK" to confirm and exit.

* NOTE: Custom Quick Access Toolbar on the right side of the page should indicate " For all documents (default).*

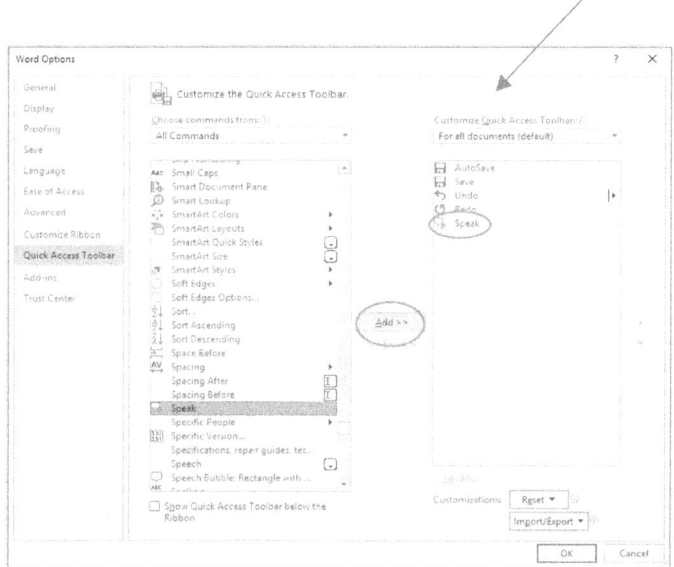

Step 7: Left click on "Review" tab and on the end, it will say " New Group" and have the Speak button as a part of the "Review" menu.

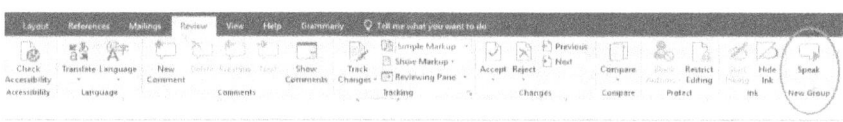

Step 8: Close Microsoft Word.

Congratulations you are set up!

HOW TO BE SURE THAT WHAT WE SETUP WORKS.

Now let's open a previous writing assignment to make sure that the function is properly working.

Open a word document of your choice and once it is displayed on your screen, go to and left click on the Review tab.

Select a section of the document and highlight it by left-clicking the text that you would like to have read. Once the text is highlighted, left-click the "Speak" button to have your selected text read aloud.

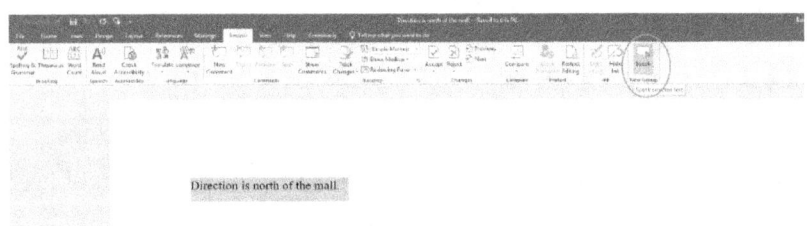

Note: The speak function will be grayed out until you highlight a section of text.

Direction is north of the mall.

The second function you will notice on this field is the "Read Aloud" button which is usually standard for newer versions of Microsoft office.

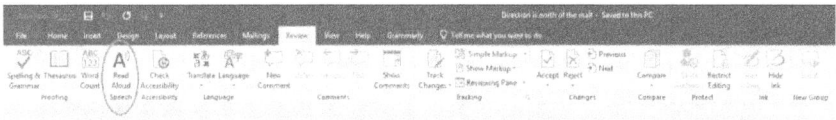

* Note the "Read Aloud" function doesn't require you to highlight the text to speak the words that are written within the document.

THE SPEAK FUNCTION VS. READ ALOUD FUNCTION

Now that you have enabled the buttons on the review tab, how do you decide on which one to use? Here are a few pros and cons for each function that you will want to keep in mind as you start to use these tools.

The "Speak" Function:

Pros

1. It allows you to highlight a section of text that you want to review in blocks rather than reading the entire document without stopping or timing out.

2. The speak function is in a voice that seems more natural to the way that I would read it. Even though this feature can be changed, the default setting was the best option.

Cons:

1. It takes a little time to enable this function rather than using something that is already enabled within the Review tab.

2. When you are reviewing projects with 10 or more pages, it could become an annoyance to constantly have to highlight the different sections just to have the text read back to you.

The "Read Aloud" Function:

Pros

1. It doesn't require you to highlight a section of text that you want to review, and it will read the text on the page from the beginning.

2. The read-aloud function is already enabled for newer versions of Microsoft word and you can begin to use the feature right away.

Cons:

1. It selects a section of text based on where the page begins rather than where you are reading, which can slow you down.

2. The voice selection and small icons to control the setting of the read-aloud features makes it difficult to read the section. It can time out or malfunction if you begin adjusting some of these features.

MY PERSONAL PREFERENCE

During my graduate program I have tried both methods, however I prefer to use the "Speak" function over the "Read Aloud" function. The speak function allows me to build each section of my paper in a way that helped me to correct errors as it read the text. Also, this function helped me ensure that the topic that I was writing about was in the tone that I wanted to convey my understanding and message to the audience.

Each person will have their preference for either of these tools, however, the most important thing is to know that you now have them available to use as a method to help you become a better writer and graduate student. Be sure to take 10 - 15 minutes to play around with these functions and customize them to your specific comfort. These tools will take your writing to the next level and allow you to catch those small errors that other people often miss.

Action Plan:

Develop a habit of using this feature to re-read your paper back to you to ensure that what you are writing is what other people are understanding. There have been countless times when I finished my paper and thought that it was completely done until I had it read back to me using these functions. Utilizing this powerful tool will allow you to stand out among your peers, and recapture points missed due to small spelling and grammatical errors. The ability to evoke all the senses during this process of writing and creating is the key to clarifying your message and effectively communicating with your audience. Let's move ahead to Writing Element 3, which will be the final writing element of this book. This section will help you to build superior writing habits and a stronger academic foundation as a result of focusing on quality rather than quantity.

GRADUATE WRITING ELEMENT 3: FOCUS ON QUALITY

"Simplicity is the Ultimate Sophistication."

– Leonardo Da Vinci (1452-1519)

As a graduate student, your ability to simplify very complex concepts requires you to focus on quality over quantity to convey a graduate level of comprehension. One of the most common mistakes that I experienced during my master's program was the fact that there were some students in my program that thought that if they wrote 15 pages of garbage that it would demonstrate a graduate level of understanding and comprehension. They assumed that bulk equaled quality and proficient writing, and it doesn't. Anyone can write 27 pages about a whole bunch of nothing to prove that they did something, but graduate school is not about writing for writing sake. At this level of education, a higher precision and focus is needed to demonstrate a level of mastery. For those that focused on volume rather than quality, the only thing that they did was waste their time and everyone else's that had to read it. Those were the students that didn't make the cut, and I didn't see them in any other classes thereafter nor on graduation day. It was rather unfortunate because many of them were great people. They just didn't have a good writing strategy in place to see it all the way through to the finish line. Therefore, this last writing element focuses on quality over quantity. This section will help you understand how to create a lot of content that is high in quality while also reaching the page requirements for a given assignment.

Most employers are looking for candidates that are able to demonstrate high proficiency in written communication skills at the college level. Businesses around the world are looking for quality writers who are able to bolster the image and profile of the organization. Writers who are able to clearly and accurately communicate their vision and mission to a worldwide audience will prove to be the most valuable within this arena. In the era of tweets, emojis, 10-second commercials, and fake news, your ability to think critically, discern truth from fiction, solve complex issues, all while communicating clearly to your peers and upper management is essential in growing as a professional.

The next sections will focus on helping you to develop the habits and skills that are needed to be a better scholar and professional. We will address structuring and formatting in the first two sections, but then we will change gears and have a detailed look at the issue of quality versus quantity. This section is particularly interesting as I reveal my 120/80 rule and go through the steps that you can use in creating your project.

Now that we are ready, let's go to Simple Habit # 7, where we address Structuring Essentials.

SIMPLE HABIT 7:
STRUCTURING ESSENTIALS

The traditional way of structuring a paper has not changed too much over the last 30 years, meaning that for most works you will have a beginning, middle, and end to your paper. In graduate school, the format is a little more detailed in that you will have a cover page, an abstract at the beginning, and reference page for the specific style of citation that is required e.g. APA, MLA. A strategy that I used involved identifying common themes that I would put in my paper that never changed e.g. the cover page. I know that I was going to finish my degree at my institution and therefore I used the same cover or title page for each of my works. The only thing that I would change is the name of the professor, the title and the date (if the date was required). Not having to construct this every time shortened the number of things that I had to type for each project. This was especially important when I had multiple assignments in different classes.

Having the ability to just copy and paste things and set up the structure of my paper on day one proved to be an invaluable resource in completing different projects for multiple classes efficiently and on time. I created templets for the title page, abstract, body paragraphs, etc. This helped me to organize and structure my paper on day one. This simple habit helped me to get something put into each of those sections as soon as the assignment was given.

For example, the title page looked like.

Heading

Your Name

School Name

Course Code: E.g. HCMA 6001

Professors Name

By having these templets pre-filled with information like name and school it will give you a great psychological boost and help you to be more prepared for the assignments.

Action Plan:

Create a file or folder for your working templates. Develop a common structure for your paper and build a template that you can copy paste into your work. By doing this, it will shorten the amount of work that you will have to do and allow for more time to focus on your content. Now, that this section is complete, let's move on to Simple Habit #8 where I can't wait to show you the order separation methodology. See you there!

SIMPLE HABIT 8:
ORDER SEPARATION

The order of separation is a method that I used during my master's degree to organize the order that I wrote my papers. This method focuses on starting the paper by writing the meat and potatoes first, and then finishing it up with the appetizer and dessert sections of the paper. For this reason, I would primarily focus on the main bodies of the paper and then I would complete the other sections afterwards. I would use the speech-to-write technology mentioned above for each section and combine that with the information that I researched to form each body paragraph. Finally, once each body paragraph is completed, then I would write the introduction, the conclusion, and the abstract last.

Do the introduction, conclusion, and abstract last?

Yes, do the introduction, conclusion, and abstract last. The introduction, conclusion, and abstract play a unique role in the construction of an academic essay, and as a result, it demands much more of your attention as a writer. The introduction states the purpose and goals of what you researched. A good introduction should identify your topic, specify your area of focus, and deliver essential context which engages the reader's interest. The conclusion is a summary of your findings and your assessment of what needs to be done as a result of your research. The abstract should be the last thing that you write, as it is a 15 second summary of your entire paper. The abstract is what helps researchers identify the key themes of your paper when they come across your work.

What is an abstract, and does every paper require one?

An abstract is a summary of points that are made throughout the written work that condenses the essential components of the overall written work. Metaphorically speaking, I think of it as the 15-second movie trailer for your paper, which gives the reader enough information so that they would want to read more of what you have written within your paper. Not every writing assignment will require that you present an abstract, however, it is important for you to familiarize yourself with its construct.

Now that you understand this strategy, the next thing you need to do is to follow the order placement methodology and action plan to make this become an effective habit.

Action Plan:

Simply hang a posted note on your computer for the order separation method and use it as a step by step guide to follow as you write your paper. Continue to reference your note until it becomes a habit. In the next section we will look at addressing some of the common misconceptions about quality vs. quantity in graduate school.

SIMPLE HABIT 9
QUALITY OVER QUANTITY

The quality versus quality debate is one that is old as time, and it is a topic that touches every segment of society including academia. This dilemma is something that you will face as you enter and continue through your graduate program. In my experience, those that are the most successful focus on quality, and it is the one factor that separates those students who excel in the program from those that are barely getting by.

So, what should I focus on, Quality or Quantity?

Well, both. However, you will need to have a higher focus on quality than quantity. Clear as mud, right?

The truth is that it will be highly contingent on the assignment and the final deliverables for that project.

The rule of thumb that I used during my master's degree is 120/80 rule. This rule is something that I discovered during my bachelor's degree, and it states that" I need to produce 120% of the volume content for an assignment to get to 80% clarity." As an example, to produce 120% in writing volume means that if an assignment required me to submit a 5-page report, automatically I would know that I would have to create at least 6 to 7 pages of content to begin to use this strategy. From there I would then refine my entire paper down to ensure that 80% of what I wanted to clearly communicate was accurately positioned within my paper.

Coincidently enough, I found that as I utilized this strategy I would either exceed the required length of the project or create the exact page requirement for the assignment.

So why 80% rather than 100% clarity?

It's because of time. Time as a graduate student can be your best friend or your worst enemy. My writing significantly improved because I wasn't trying to create more content at the last minute before an assignment was due. Rather my strategy focused on simply refining my work to improve the clarity and punctuation of what I had written.

Action Plan:

Use the strategies that you have learned in previous chapters to create your content and then use the 120/80 rule to ensure that the quality and quantity reflects the requirements for your written assignment. Practice this strategy and it will become one of your most powerful writing habits as a graduate student.

Finally, we have arrived at the final habit. In this section, I reveal a powerful key to your success. Let's go ahead to the next section where this special key awaits you!

SIMPLE HABIT 10:
YOUR SPECIAL KEY TO SUCCESS

The key to success that I have found over the years is to remain focused on being the best version of myself and making it a goal to get a little better at something positive every day. Handling feedback and criticism was one of the greatest lessons that I learned about success during my time in the military. Throughout my experience, I learned how not to take feedback as a personal attack but instead use it as a guide to improve different areas of my life and career. My advice to you is that you become the type of person that is receptive to feedback from other scholars and professors that offer you help.

The one thing that I didn't realize for most of my life was the fact that asking for help isn't a sign of weakness, but it is a sign of strength. No one person has a monopoly on knowledge, the motto of seek and you shall find is eternal. Be someone who is known for always seeking knowledge and self-improvement, then success will follow.

For what is life but the mastery of self. Be a master of one (you) and not of all. The thing that you bring to the world is your light. You are the secret!

Action Plan:

Find a writing mentor. This can be a professor, a librarian, a professional writer, etc., and work to create a genuine relationship with them. These people are usually very willing to help you and mentor you, and if they are not, find someone else, no worries. Realize that everyone who is good at a thing is not always great at being a teacher. Make it a habit to continue reaching out to people, whether that is on social media or in person, focus on those that want to work with you to help you improve your writing. Work to set up your professional network within the first 30 days after reading this book. Write down all of your educational and career goals and achieve them.

CLOSING COMMENTS

"Life Isn't About Finding Yourself.
Life is About Creating Yourself. "
- George Bernard Shaw (1865-1950)

Embrace the journey and learn as much as you can. Start to create the best version of you and take the time to invest in building yourself up and creating your legacy because you are worth it! For what is life but a journey to mastery of ones' self. The light that you will create from being the best version of you can illuminate the world and influence others to make that positive change to become a better writer, a better student, a better teacher, a better parent, a better scholar. Always remember to let your inner light shine brightly.

I want to thank you again for purchasing this book and taking your initial steps towards becoming a better writer!

I anticipate your future success and I hope that I was able to provide you with an effective methodology in creating the perfect graduate paper. With these powerful habits, you will be able to effectively communicate your message to any audience and shine like the star that you are.

The next step for you is to use the strategies in this book to refine your writing to make it better with each assignment. Please let me know exactly how effective these strategies are in conquering your fears and anxiety about writing at the graduate level.

If you enjoyed this book, could you please take 20 seconds to share your positive thoughts and post a review on the Amazon book page! I would really appreciate your feedback as it helps spread the word about my work.

Thank you so much! **Love is Love**.

PS: Please feel free to e-mail me at AB.Writing.Method@gmail.com this is my personal email address with your questions. Know that you will receive a response as I reply to every email that I receive!

Also, remember to pick up the ** *FREE BONUS CONTENT*** over at www.graduatewriting.club where you can join my e-mail list to remain connected to current events, newsletters, exclusive bonus content, and free discounts on future products!

www.ingramcontent.com/pod-product-compliance
Lightning Source LLC
Chambersburg PA
CBHW071243280526
45788CB00004B/1557